Go-Karting

Written by
Jill Atkins

Ransom

Were you looking for a fun sport to do?

Well, you might have a crack at go-karting.

There might be a track near you.
Go there if you can.

Go-karting is the sort of thing
you can do just for fun.

Or you can train and
get some better skills.

Then you might turn
into the best!

You will need all
the gear.

This might all cost
a lot, but you can
rent this stuff with
a go-kart.

Do not forget
the helmet.

Some go-karts have a bar at the back, to stop you getting hurt if you flip.

Some go-karts have a lot of power and are quick.

Go-karts for teens and kids have less power. This is so that they do not crash the kart on the track.

You have to plug some go-karts in to get power.

This plug-in kart is terrific. Is it a hot rod?

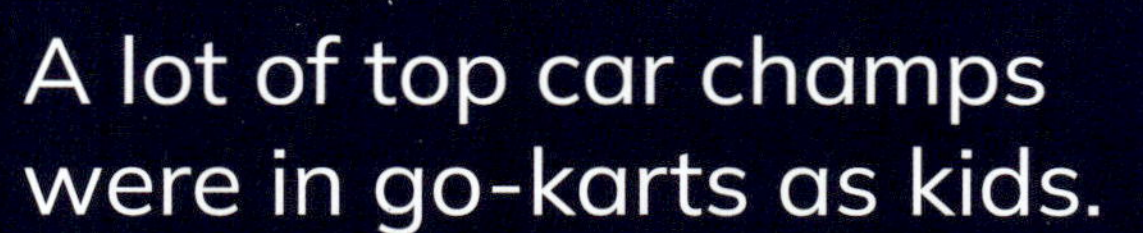

A lot of top car champs were in go-karts as kids.

Some of them were
go-kart champs then,
and are car champs now.

Will she be a champ too?